Love Surrounded Me

Poems and Songs

by

Cindy Loggins Hale

Keithley Creek Publishing
2018

Keithley Creek Publishing, LLC
2275 Keithley Creek Road
Midvale, ID 83645

www.keithleycreek.com

keithleycreek@gmail.com

Cover & Text Design by: Cindy Hale

A CIP record for this book is acailable from the Library of Congress Cataloging-in-Publication Data

ISBN-eBook: 978-1-7322412-7-5

ISBN- Print: 978-1-7322412-4-4

Distributed by:

Ingram Content Group, Inc.
One Ingram Blvd.
La Vergne, TN 37086
Printed and bound in United States by Ingram Spark

Dedicated to

Great-Grandma Eunice Owen

(1873-1960)

Whose writing and art created one hundred years before me – and careful preservation of the same - led me to writing and art as a means of expressing myself.

Grandma, the kinship I felt with you
as I was privileged to read and enjoy your poems,
drawings and stories describing your life
helped me to see the beauty in things around me.
Stories I heard about you – although we never met–
helped me appreciate my blessings, even in dark days.
For example, your courage in moving across the country in 1931, when hope shone from afar, helped me have courage to make a similar move in 2003-2004 when it became necessary.

As I wrote and composed my own words, I found relief, preserved memories and learned deeper lessons, impossible on a shallower level, which sustained me through difficulty.
Your careful preservation of family heirlooms
- and relationships -
inspires me to this day to preserve and build the best I can,
in all things.

Your love has always surrounded me.

Contents

Foreword

My daughter confidently informed me at 18: "If God wanted me to blend in, He would not have made me smart, red-haired and 6'2". Similarly endowed, I did not blend in well, either, with the Southern California culture into which I was born - but unfortunately did not have her early wisdom. Rejections and traumatic events, small and large, simply festered painfully for me, accumulating in a fractured, waxy burden that took a long time to clear and heal. Developing a thicker skin has taken me half a century.

One way I found of dealing with both my difficulties and the beautiful and compensating revelations of faith over the years was through journaling, sometimes writing poetry. Through writing, I was able to preserve my own thoughts and feelings, so they were not lost in the abyss of daily immediacy and others' overpowering personalities. Writing was one thread tying me to self when fatigue, sorrow and more than twenty years of hidden domestic violence nearly erased me entirely.

Thus, the tone of these poems ranges from cheerful to sorrowful, sarcastic to sublime. It seems best to categorize them by when they were written. Enough time has passed that they can be shared without too much discomfort.

Leaving out the snarky, edgy ones would make the whole incomplete. So, there you have it. Rather than judge, consider those a hand outstretched to those who are struggling with similar challenges.

Thanks for reading.

1990s

In the late 1980s, I wanted more sheet music to play on the piano, but our budget was too tight to accommodate such things. So, I thought I would write some new songs and arrangements myself. It was so satisfying, and I felt it was a wonderful way to express my faith and thoughts. So, I continued. In about 1992, I began adding lyrics.

My already difficult marriage deteriorated badly in this decade, despite my very best efforts and focus. I had been taught all my life that marriage was sacred, something to apply one's very best efforts to, something one must not give up on, no matter what. Spiritually, I ran on fumes, dealing almost daily with harsh criticism, even violence, that, of course, wore down my defenses in a putrid mix of confusion and shame. It was a nightmare, to put it bluntly, and yet I felt my path was to stay and try to make things work. What that faithfulness and devotion cost me, no one but God knows.

During the worst times, towards the end, we lived in a place with space for gardening and a lovely old fruit orchard planted by my father-in-law. The pastoral beauty of the garden and orchard was the source of much peace and joy in that turbulent period.

In 1995, at an emotional low point, I began a wonderful, satisfying association with the Arrowhead Chapter of the California Federation of Chaparral Poets. Our group provided much-needed encouragement; bolstering my confidence, shaping my style, and providing an opportunity to share – and excel. I began to see myself and my work more objectively and was amazed to find commonality among these people. Some were real characters. I met wonderful people, including writer and activist Eldridge Cleaver and author Ray Bradbury, and all of the talented and kindly poets and writers of Chaparral, who are still my good friends.

There was Alice – a true and lasting friend, an accomplished writer, historian and teacher. There was June – a most free-spirited, positive individual, a true lover of the written word. There was gentle Myrna – recovering as I was from trauma and finding hope in written expression. There was Dorothy – bright and cheerful despite trials, and full of amazing ideas and connections. There was Loretta, whose thoughtful, funny poetry on motherhood and cheerful practicality debunked the false expectations under which I labored. There was Cindy – poet, quilter and fabric artist, close to my age, with a son in the same school.

There was Al – dear, rule-observant Al, whose devotion to his wife (whom he called "my queen") touched me deeply. And there was Lily, whose education, adherence to form and willingness to teach helped me to welcome her comments on my work – because they really helped me improve.

Oh, and I cannot forget the brothers Green, dressed in their dark pinstripe suits and white brimmed hats – all over town. And a sweet fellow, an independent adult who had been born and raised in an insane asylum. Each was special, an angel sent to help me on my way.

Creator's Child (1992)

To know the Creator who gave us birth
Till and toil and tame the Earth –
Our Heavenly Father's love of creation
Is starting to grow in me.

We till the soil and we plant the seeds,
We tend the fruits and we pull the weeds;
A little water is all that this lovely flower needs.
    Even in a pot, there's life!
    I can be creator in my yard
    Blessings of the body and the mind,
    Following a prophet's guide.

Life lessons manifest to you and me:
Reading the Holy Scriptures we can see
Pruning and nurturing are principles of necessity.
    Even in a pot, there's life!
    I can be creator in my yard
    Blessings of the body and the mind,
    Following a prophet's guide.

Gardens, in miniature, are worlds-to-be,
We practice as we fill our daily needs.
As children playing house, we learn as we do,
    Eternally.

The Golden Cup (1992)

I need the hope to carry on
The blessed light that shines at dawn
I'll turn to the Scriptures, they're written for me,
Daily study will bring peace.

    They will comfort you, they will teach you truth.
    Open the books: find and feel the love there is for you.

I love the books, the holy ones.
They testify of God's own Son,
His words and His life, they have answers for me;
Emulating Him brings peace.

    He will comfort you, He will teach you truth.
    Open the books: find and feel the love He has for you.

Eternity speaks from the dust;
A golden cup, filled to the brim
With Living Water, the pure light of Christ
Who died and lives for me.
He says to me
    "I will comfort you, I will teach you truth.
    Open the books: find and feel the love I have for you."

A Love Born of Faith (1995)

Searching for you, watching the sky,
For the love that I always knew was coming;
I was ready to see, to live and to be
All eternity yours – and I knew when I saw you.
The altar we knelt at, the clothes that I wore,
And the flowers I held in my hands,
In my memory always I treasured.
The journey that started so balmy and sweet-
Fierce storms did arise. How we trembled and strove!
Inexperience brought us down to our knees,
And our trials began.
Storm after storm came,
Blinded and tired, we struggled along
Blundered together in rightness and wrong.
We stayed, slow and lagging, on the caravan trail.
Often we doubted, when the fire was hot,
Whether love's light was still in our hearts.
Yet we pressed on, we pressed on!
We knew not how else to honor the Lord
Who had joined us together.
We stepped forward, rising each time that we fell.
And sometimes, in calm times,
When the waves ceased to crash,
Our faith in the love that we shared

Was rewarded by joy.
We discovered that laughter and love in our family
Tempered the voices of sorrow and pain;
And discouragement, grumbling,
Left as we followed our Savior and King.
Then when the Refiner
Had taught us to see
The perspective of God,
Our hearts yearned to sing!
When we were unable,
Through grim, misted lies
To reach out to each other
For nourishment, wise
Was our Father, who taught me to see
That by faith's tender touch
And the Spirit's assistance
I could see and receive
What I needed so much.
A wonderful love, newly flourishing, grew,
Faith as my companion and friend has become;
Faith in our Savior, faith in His love,
Faith in forgiveness,
And faith in a wonderful, beautiful you.

Apricot (1996)

Delicious
Ripe fruit of my labors,
I bite and slurp your soft sweetness,
Your heaven-kissed flavor
Like sunshine on my tongue.

Christmas Time (1996)

In absence of required funds to send a shiny gift,
How 'bout I send a sappy poem to lend a loving lift?

Christmas time comes, and we reflect
On our precious family ties;
We check our emotional safety net
And realize time flies.
Friends and foes may come and go,
But family ties remain.
They reach beyond distance and circumstance;
Our inner souls they frame.
We share the days that came before,
The lives and loves that make us kin;
Brothers, sisters, cousins and more
Were some of our childhood friends.
Naturally, our hearts reach to the past
When we think of what we want to be.
And when I do this, I am glad
That you're related to me.
I have a pleasant memory
Of every one of you.
But life goes on – we all are changed
By everything we do.
Chances are, you wouldn't know me
If I walked by you in the street.

But I might not know you either –
Some I may never meet!
So, now it seems it's up to us
To preserve the memories
You may find unexpected friends
Lurking in family trees.
There's part of me in all of you,
There's part of you in me.
What more is there that we can do
To strengthen our family?
Accept the weakness with the strength
That you can see in me,
I'll do the same, we both will know
More strength in unity.
Sorrows are lighter and joys are greater
When shared by your family.
Just do what you can – you're all welcome
To write or come see me.
Tornado Alley's what it looks like here
With cats, dogs, five kids and three geese,
An acre of fruit trees and pastures –
It's really a kid's paradise.
Some even call me "Ma Kettle,"
Music and books are my friends,
But you and I could talk a while
Before this journey ends.

In God's Hands (1996)

O Father!
This turn of events reveals
My trembling timidity,
My wavering weakness of soul.
The pendulating balance seeks its rest...
Will my effort be enough?

I strive for the solid strength and flexibility
Of a well-oiled faith,
The masterful maintenance of discipline,
And the unwearying alloy of adoration
That Thy true instrument must possess.
My insufficiency is yet offset by Thy mercy,
Thy gentle finger on the scale!

How kind Thou art
To Thy unprofitable children!
I will reflect this kindness,
And be grateful for the refining fire
That makes me Thine.

Kingdom Contrast (1996)

Living weakness,
Clouded joy;
Measured marvels,
Lonely noise.
Mighty trembling
Here you see --
Life in telestiality.

Wondrous sparrows,
Fruited trees,
Graceful branches
Family.
Soul-filled yearning
Calmly burning
Celestial pleasure
Without measure.

My Teacher, My Waterbearer (1996)

For my parents and others

You fed me – a hungry, thirsty soul –
With nuggets of truth
And great draughts of Living Water.
Patiently, for much was dropped or wasted,
You bore my numerous misadventures,
My pains of sorrow, my flickering faith;
And waited for that precious moment
When my soul was open, ready to hear,
Sufficiently nourished, in its many needs,
To listen.
Then, lovingly, you applied your energy
To helping me see, and more importantly,
To feel
The immense undergirding of Love,
That great Foundation
Upon which to build my own house of faith
In which I will live my life.
You illustrated the importance of action
As building material,
Because a house of straw –
Of shallow purpose, of fleeting interest - -
Is rarely shelter in the storm of life.
My walls begin to brick up nicely now;
I shelter and feed others as I can.
I see what you did, and oh, it is not easy.

I thank you.

Picnic Vision (1996)

After a February church conference in Palm Springs

Beneath
Majestic mountain grandeur,
Brilliant yet gentle sun
Illuminates the shady lawns;
The silken blossoms rejoicing,
The very leaves
Turning their hearts to the Light!
Immaculate avenues
Lead to the joyful gathering
Of friends and family, united:
Peaceable refreshment
Available to all.

Remembering Eunice Owen (1996)

From Meriden, Kansas;
Prairie maid schoolteacher
Bright and witty, yet subdued
Daughter of a Union soldier -
Founder of this tiny town on wide horizons -
And a determined pioneer mother.
Born as you were the week your older sister died,
Your mother must have held you tightly;
Your father called you Puny-Eunie.
As your great-granddaughter, I must say
I am glad you lived
Not only for my own life,
But also, for your artist's heart,
And your sweetly bowed lips
That grace my daughter's face.
She is eight, and much like you.
I see you that age,
Smoothing your calico dress
As you settle in the shade
To draw and paint wildflowers
That vaunt in the sun,
Brushing a gnat away.

Stage Fright (1996)

Shiver-quiveringly, my knees
Question the need
To bear my weight:
I must scold them firmly –
And my cold, palsied hands, my fluttering brain,
Like unruly children
Who chase and fight when recess is over.
The schoolteacher
Must blow her whistle – several times!
Before they reluctantly form a line,
Elbowing each other slyly,
And march.

The Evidence (1996)

There are the facets of love:
The gleam of memory
On centenarian face;
Two become one;
The hand of a baby;
The adoration of a child;
The quiet answer;
Shared work, joy and sorrow;
Friendship.
And the living Earth:
Creeping, crumbling fertility
Begetting infinite variety
And nourishment for all;
A moonlit orchard,
Softly twittered birds' greetings;
The light of dawn
Gliding over the mountain,
And the dewy stillness that precedes it;
Quiet waters, roaring surf;
Melting snow, gentle rain
Echoing, cleansing on a roof of tin;
Shimmering ripples of wind on grass;
Wide canyons, deep with secrets
From antiquity.
God loves.
God knows.

Waiting on the Lord (1996)

Whispers of the Spirit speak of comfort,
Peace to my faint, trembling heart,
Oh Lord!
   I will do, I will be
   All that Thou wouldst have of me.
   Thou art near, ever near;
   Oh, how can I express my thanks to Thee,
   Praise to Thee?
In the morning calm I praise Thee,
Gently comes Thy answering Hope.
Oh Lord!
   I will do, I will be
   All that Thou wouldst have of me.
   Thou art near, ever near;
   Oh how can I express my thanks to Thee,
   Praise to Thee?
Thou hast shown to me Thy will,
And Thou art ever wise.
Lord, I will hearken and obey in faith.
In the day, and in the night,
My heart will rest to know that Thou art right.
In the dark, and in the light,
Ever faithful Thou wilt find me
Waiting on the Lord.

Baptism of a Child (1997)

Father, I am here at the water's edge.
I want to come now, come into the fold of God.
Leaving all my sins, may I come to Thee now,
In a new life?
What a wonder!
Through the love of my Savior,
Someday I can live with Thee,
Someday I can be like Thee!
It all starts right here at the water's edge.
I am ready to enter Thy fold.

Willing to bear another's burden,
And to comfort and mourn with those in need.
To witness of God, even 'til death.
To be numbered with the first in the Resurrection,
And to have the blessings of eternal life!
Dear Father, I will honor Thee, I'll be faithful,
Today I am coming to Thee.
I come to Thee, I come to Thee.

A Mother's Love (1997)

A mother's life is spent preventing harm,
Attention to all needs demanding,
Yet in the shelter of her loving arms is my security.
A mother's heart encompasses her own
And also, every child in need;
The seeds of motherhood and love are sown
In every kindly deed.
A mother's love is always,
A granite wall, a tender, fragrant rose.
Imperfect, beautiful and brave,
Thank God for the mother He chose.

A mother's strength is often said to be
A legend leading all her family,
And in her daily walk a mother's led to build a history.
A mother's soul inspires decency,
Beyond the grave her love lies surely.
When disappointment, trials and sorrows come,
The love she taught us glows.
A mother's love is always,
A granite wall, a tender, fragrant rose.
Imperfect, beautiful and brave,
Thank God for the mother He chose.

As I Teach Aisha (1997)

Thoughtful introspection,
Serious consideration,
Blossoming faith:
She is four years old,
But her eyes speak of eons of experience.
In showing her the simplest truth
I am teaching myself.

California Winter (1997)

Observations from my morning walks at Cal State

Grey-white trunks of liquidambar
Standing tall along my way
Branches arching graceful fingers
On a crisp November day.
    Why, I wonder, are you sprouting
    Leaves of green among the red?
    Could California winter fool you,
    University-born and bred?
You stand here on a college campus,
I'm amazed at your confusion!
You have foot-long shoots of green leaves
On every branch and in profusion!
    Oh now, trees, you must consider –
    February frosts yet come;
    Cold and biting winds will blow here
    Making your green branches numb.
Perhaps your roots are overwatered
Perhaps El Nino comes, you know;
Maybe excess fertilizer
Stimulates your leaves to grow,
    Grey-white trunks of liquidambar
    Standing tall along my way
    Branches arching graceful fingers
    On a crisp November day.

Early April Morning (1997)

Earth's greening tree
Dark morning, still
Misted, blooming lee,
Silent, sleeping bee
On lonely hill.

The birds still slept,
All eyes were closed
Save with One newly left,
In linen kept,
And He arose.

Soft desert dawn,
Mourned loved ones seen –
Wretched death is gone!
Eternal bonds
Life's love serene.

His glory rise,
His power and might
Are, in His wise
And glorious eyes
Our Father's right.

In quiet awe
Before Him bow.
His will our law;
Our pains He saw –
Sees our need now.

Little Stream (1997)

Trickling, burbling
Eddying in small pools,
Peaceful in its quietness;
Satisfies small appetites,
Refreshes squirrels and doves
When God's judgement rains down
Bold lightning flashes
Little stream becomes a waterfall
Carelessly sloshing, raging
To and fro, side to side,
Racing in a mad scramble
To the canyon floor.
Beautiful, yes.
Yet when the sun shines again
That sweet and silent scene returns
And heals my hurried heart
Trickling, burbling
Eddying in small pools
Refreshing squirrel and dove
Satisfying small appetites
Quiet,
Peaceful.

Through A Glass Door (1997)

One dreary, drawn-out day,
Life's gentle caresses remained:
A child's sparkle,
The radiant warmth and strength of the sun,
Yet emptiness hung about
Like a hungry dog I had fed once
And could not chase away.
My cupboard was bare.
Then suddenly,
As I stepped through the glass door,
The Spirit brought to my mind
The memory
Of concern in your eyes
The comfort of your presence
The knowledge of your love,
As invisible, yet as real
As the summer breeze.
My reservoir suddenly overflowed
Through my eyes,
And strength filled my stride.

Truth (1997)

Inflexible, biting ignorance
Disdains the truth
As some foreign monster,
Some alien force,
Whose inconvenience and unpopularity
Make it a seething enemy
Fit only for violent destruction.
Yet, truth remains –
Constant as the sun,
Immovable, comforting to those
Who seek shelter where there is none
From hurled stones,
From ungenerous misunderstanding,
From willful, knowing hatred.
Truth glows, directs
Like a candle in the night,
A warm balustrade
As one climbs eternal stairs
In the dark.
One would be wise to hang on.

Your Eyes (1997)

Your eyes, my dear, speak so clearly
That you hardly need a mouth;
Delight, desire, disappointment
And naughty glee
Are as plain on your face
As the fragrance in a tuna can.
Please don't let your tongue disagree!

Earthquake Fun (1998)

Our city lies atop a fault
San Andreas by name.
Earthquakes frighten many folks
To Mom they are a game.
For forty years she's ridden quakes
At home, outside, at work;
When estimating Richter scale
She is most alert.
First the distant roar is heard,
Then it shakes the glass;
Then the walls and heaters jump
Until the tremblings pass.
Sometimes quakes come at 3 am;
The cat can rock the bed
Just curled up tight between your feet
Or purring near your head.
A four is barely noticed now,
But when it's five-point-five
She's ready and observant,
Her senses come alive.
"A six! A six-point-five!" she says,
Hushing all the talk;
You can always tell a seven
When the clothes rack starts to rock.
She listens close for mishaps
Among her family;
She pauses in the hall to hear
The saucepan symphony.
The trembles slow, the shakes subside
Excitement's gone, and then
Mama puts aside the fun

'Til an earthquake comes again.

Mama Bear (1998)

My teens and tweens
Whisper urgently behind their hands
I hear snatches of "Don't" and "Mom"
Oh, if they only knew how recently, how recently
I played the game of cover and hide.
Great fun, yes.
Discussing who likes whom
Is never quite so interesting
As when done in secret.
It unsettles me, though,
To recall news reports
Of far less innocent subjects.
I turn my back to them
And listen intently.

Sickbed (1998)

Sluggish aches and fatigue
Make it hard work just lying in bed.
I can't sleep, but it's just as well.
If I did, I would dream of things
Like spinning heads, walking on the ceiling.
My brain reeling, I awake from a doze
To see something moving on the pillow
Beneath my eye.
A tiny, determined mealworm
From a stashed box of crackers under the bed.
I flick him expertly against the wall, and roll over,
But he rallies himself to the challenge
And creeps upward, unseen
I doze and roll again to find him
Toiling bravely
At precisely eye level.
Impressed by his fortitude,
I watch.

The Least of These (1998)

Lord, I don't want to, but I will
Oh, I don't want to, but I will.
Why is it needed?
Can't someone else love,
Someone else go today?
But I know:
Inasmuch as ye have done it
Unto the last of these my brethren
My brethren, my brethren!
Ye have done it unto me.
Oh Savior, Oh Savior, Savior
Yes, but they're dirty, ragged and foul,
Boring and bitter, please tell me how,
How can I serve them.
How can I see them with your eyes today?
I look in their eyes, I make them smile –
I see you! I love them!
Opening up thy pure love, it warms me,
It overflows.
Happiness anchors now.
We're peaceful, free and filled.
Inasmuch as ye have done it
Unto the least of these my brethren,
My brethren, my brethren!
Ye have done it unto me.
Inasmuch as ye have done it
Unto the least of these my brethren,
My brethren, my brethren!
Ye have done it unto me.

The Orchard (1998)

In pantoum form – thanks to Lilly McCue

My moonlit grove, so peaceful, gently still...
My quiet refuge, waiting ever near
To quiet my emotions, firm my will
To speak my secrets only God can hear...

My quiet refuge, waiting ever near
In nighttime hours the branches call to me,
To speak my secrets only God can hear...
Embracing me in comfort I can't see.

In nighttime hours the branches call to me,
Each waving leaf arrayed in silver glow,
Embracing me in comfort I can't see
And gentle courage once again I know.

Each waving leaf arrayed in silver glow,
List'ning, flying in the starry winds,
And gentle courage once again I know,
So comforted among my tallest friends

List'ning, flying in the starry winds,
To quiet my emotions, firm my will,
So comforted among my tallest friends
My moonlit grove, so peaceful, gently still...

William (1998)

Gentle heart, young son,
The resilience of youth is your preservation.
Grubby knees and grimy fingers,
Mud, kitty and dog slobber wash off in the tub,
Revealing your freckled peachy cheeks
That frame a gapped smile.
Cheerfully chuckling, then
Gleefully giggling
You tell of animal antics in the orchard;
There's nothing more fun than listening to you!

A Good Place (1999)

Populated by people
Looking for something better
San Bernardino, California
Its native inhabitants
Its Mormon emigrants
Who shared their produce
Its railroaders, agriculturalists
Who began our transportation system,
Planted our orchards
Even outlaws
Considered it a good place
A hub, a steppingstone
To greater things, to greater heights
An academy of sorts
Dust Bowlers, castoffs, the unfortunate
The generous, the industrious, the idealists
The entrepreneurs, the soldiers
The independent.
Perhaps even now, in spite of heat or smog
Or crime or neighborhoods in the latter cycle of life
We share a common heritage of ambition
We share the responsibility to lift in some way
Those who arrived after we did.
In the way we conduct our business, our lives
We owe it to those before who did more with less
And had the courage
To stay and build.

Alphabet (1999)

Able Babies Can Do Everything
Frail Guppies Hide In Jars
Killer Leeches Meet Near Oceans
Poets Quantify Remarkably Simple Terms
Unreasonably Vocal Wannabees eXist
Yielding Zilch

Answers (1999)

A thousand violins, a million flutes
Could not sing as sweetly or with such energy
As soul-strumming answers to heartfelt prayer.

Composing (1999)

Composing is
A delicate golden cage
To tame the fleeting bird of memory
Which daily grows more beautiful.

Floors (1999)

In the crazy mix of order and disorder that is my life
I try to write.
Dappled sunny tree-shadows dance
Upon the dusty couch.
At least the floors are clean.
You always know it's time to mop
When your feet stick.
It's quiet now – they're running in the orchard
But in a minute, a vocal Vesuvius will erupt,
You can be sure.
Squealing, squirting, squawking, shouting,
Shalumphing across the wood floors
Like a herd of elephants.
I grew up on concrete.
Did we ever make this much noise?
They're bonking, bashing, bantering,
Bragging, bawling, beautiful children
But I yell to quiet them – real smart!
At least the floor is clean.

Mommy Time (1999)

Close the window, clear the floor,
Turn the tap, begin to dream,
Seal the crack beneath the door
To muffle distant thump and scream.

Lost in drifting clouds of steam,
My mind at rest, my poems flow –
But of a sudden, it would seem,
Little William has to go.

My water's cold now (way to go)
The dishwasher's used up all the hot;
The kids are lined up in a row;
A perfect bath time this is not.

One Night (1999)

God unlocked my heart one night
As I sat alone on a shiny mauve davenport
That hugged the floor;
Three locks were opened.
Life looks different now.

Strength (1999)

Daunting discouragement trembles
When faith and action combine.
"No more!" cries my soul;
I pursue.

Faith's pure constant stream
Degenerates doubt's crumbling granite
Into drifts of dust.
I persist.

Calibration – cheerful,
Continued carrying on - -
Becomes celebration!
I prevail.

Thoughts While Canning (1999)

Bottled emotional pain
Is prone to spiritual botulism,
Exploding moldy jars
Full of microbial anger, bitterness;
Opened, spewing a putrid stench -
Or hidden poison.

But –

Preserved with purifying forgiveness
Sweetened with faith and love,
Memories pour forth
Beautiful, nourishing feasts
Of colors and feelings
Improved with age.

Three Friends (1999)

Her friends came –
Three standing together
To guide and counsel me
In preparation.

They came again today
To remind me, to gently tell
It is not far
Have faith.

I wonder why they come.
Such good friends they must be.
When they come again, I want
To tell them I listened.

2000s

As a very big gate turns on a very small hinge, the 2000s were characterized by drastic and irreversible events set into motion by small long-ago decisions. As I grew in faith and confidence, and no longer cowered in fear and anger, I was faced with greater and greater criticism and violence, now frequently in the presence of others. Often in such situations, things get worse before they get better. The chips fell where they fell, however, and a miraculous path was laid out that carried me out of the reach of my tormentor.

Visions sustained me through the most difficult times. In one, described in the title of this book, I was riding a bus home from work through a neighborhood riddled by violence. My six-year-old son was with me, as child care options were nil and my boss was understanding. Suddenly something hit the side of the bus; gunshots were heard, and faraway shouting. People on the bus were tense and afraid. Someone screamed. But, as though my son and I were in a cocoon of love, I was completely at peace. I saw kind blue eyes in my mind and felt immense, intense peace and assurance all around me. I knew all would be well. Love surrounded me so intensely at that moment. I knew my every worthy desire would be answered in full. My grown son remembers this event, and we marvel now.

I lay awake far into the night one evening, crying desperately to God for relief from a bitter sense of failure and disappointment. So much was going wrong, and the stress was overwhelming. I had cried myself out, praying all the while, when a bird began singing the most beautiful song outside my window around 2:30 am. I listened, letting the beauty of it wash over me. The unseen angel sang gloriously and continually, soothing my burnt-out loneliness and sorrow with heavenly grace, singing me to sleep with his lovely lullaby. Night after night, for about two weeks, he came, singing deep into the dark, silent night. I felt surrounded and assured once again with the love of God, sustaining me through this excruciating time.

My five amazing children began leaving the nest in this decade, which is perhaps the hardest part of mothering. They have never wandered far in their hearts, for which I am grateful – despite my very real challenges in healing. In 2003-2004, I was led to move to Idaho, more than 900 miles away - and my dear parents moved with me, selling their home of 38 years.

A long period of uncomfortable healing ensued, aided immeasurably by crainio-sacral therapy and other unfamiliar, intense alternative methods, rooting out the deep layers of trauma accumulated over the years. Real growth, I have learned, is always uncomfortable. So, I am grateful. How blessed I was to find compassionate, competent care at this critical time. I was blessed by working, going to school and staying active in church – despite continuing challenges. I continued to write but missed the support I had found with Chaparral.

Opportunities to date occurred, but I was blessed – or plagued - with the ability to love just about anyone – as everyone seemed so wonderful after what I had been through. Fortunately, I was cautious.

After a period of healing, growing, learning and observing, I better understood what I needed in a companion. The poems in *this* book stop at that point.

Heavenly blessing and timing, along with careful consideration, led me to Lowell, whom I met ten years ago this summer. His kind, gentle ways and enduring family focus reminded me of the love of God, and his blue eyes felt like coming home to me. He has brought more peace into my life than I have ever experienced and has taught my children, by his example, what a peaceful home is made of. He was – and is – the only person I ever met who does not drain my energy, but adds to and increases it, just by being himself. I often say he is worth every single pain I endured. Perhaps I will write more about him in the next book.

Cindy Loggins Hale
May 2018

New Year's Day 2000 (2000)

Purple sunrise beckons
A day of vision and hope;
A day like – yet unlike – any other.
Our reckoning affords us the opportunity
To see a fresh beginning,
To shed old habits, start anew
To praise God more purely,
Develop talents more diligently,
Serve God and man more willingly
In wisdom and order.

Alfie's Thrift Store (2000)

I dropped into Alfie's the other day:
Antique dolls line the walls,
Next to doilies and tin
And wacky contraptions to put your stuff in.
Rows of dull books yield occasional finds
Just walking through here comforts my mind.
Old linens and sheets are on display
Near the needles and yarn for those who crochet.
I see the old Dairy Queen each time I park.
I once bought two cowbells here, on a lark,
A small kitchen shelf, some other things –
But happy pink Sixties' doodads and rings
Don't bring me in here.
It's memories
Of love and fun in days gone by
In Great-Aunt Ethel's old house nearby.

Are You Listening? (2000)

Are you listening?
You may hear soft hellos
And whispered sighs,
When disappointment's glare
Or bereft solitude weigh heavily;
When luminescent stars appear
On weary evenings
Or in predawn hours
When the candle must burn.

Great-Aunt Hazel's old treadle sewing machine worked about as well as the electric version – and much more quietly.
A friend's similar experience with a push mower follows.

Cordless (2000)

Treadling seamstress
Smirks inwardly,
Content.
Why did they make them electric?

Low Maintenance (2000)

Pushing the gleaming blades,
He impresses the neighbors;
But, curiously,
It is in calculating total drops
Of sweat expended
That the gas mower loses.

Genealogy (2000)

Joining generations generates joy.
Push the button, computer hums,
Excitement – a new link!
The struggles of a soul
Summarized in bits and bytes of email.
Welcome stranger – father, mother –
We remember you!
Are you watching, waiting beyond the wall,
Wishing you had written more
When hands and spirit were yet one?
Never mind.
We will find
All that is to be had,
And you can tell us the rest
When we meet.

Life's Highway (2000)

Along life's bumpy, lovely road
I travel through the years;
Any way that I may go
The road is paved with tears.
Tears of sorrow, tears of joy,
Sunrises, sunsets;
Jagged mountains I must climb
Rest stops of tenderness.
How shall I choose the best road
And find happiness inside?
A wise man said the best way
Is to thank God for the ride,
Place my hand in His and work
So cheerfully each day
That happiness sneaks up behind
And sunbeams come to play.
As I bravely meet each turn
With patience and a smile,
I can lift and ease another's way
Bringing peace each mile.

Cowbells (2000)

What is there to like about cowbells?
Rusty, ugly, cloddish things –
But seeing them in the thrift store
I snatch, collect and love them.
Perhaps the clunky tinkle
Speaks to me of pastoral charm,
Of new-mown hay,
Of beauty in ugliness,
Or the grace in ungainly walks.
Perhaps the clinking collar reminds me
Of the great Shepherd
Who, if I am faithful,
Will not let me wander too far.

Faithful Lawn Chair (2000)

Worn wooden lawn chair,
You return to my porch
Each time I discard you,
Your frame I should torch.

Designed in a time
When utility reigned,
You bear my poundage
With all that I've gained.

With silky construction
And a seat that's not frayed,
You still hold together-
So you've got it made.

Picnic (2000 and 2004)

Sprrt! Opens soda;
Glistening, charred franks
Exuding garlicky perfume
Sizzle.

Potato chips,
Salty, rich, oozing flavor,
Crisp, delightsome crunch:
Sucking yields longer pleasure
Until morning weigh-in, anyway.

Napoleon Complex (2000)

Dear Josephine:

I do not know

What mental twist

Brings you to mind,

But your existence,

Long ago

Helps me

A little comfort find.

Patience (2000)

Patience
Is not the same as waiting:
I feel nothing but impatience when I wait.
Patience rechannels focus and energy
To align readiness
With balance and wisdom.

Prince Douglas (2000)

Singed ambition, frayed fortitude,
Plastic pleasure, mellowed spark;
I'm near exhaustion, but I'm grateful
That you lie near me at dark.

You're my prince, my lord, my lover
Though at meals you belch and fart;
Others' words and fancy trapments
Do not sway my loving heart.

It seems sometimes that you must hate me:
Madness raging bitter blows
Of words heartfelt or rashly spoken
Saying thus – and yet you know

That you and I in timeless pleasure
Far away among the stars
Could see and feel all truth around us
Knowing all the joys there are.

Quickie (2000)

I'm writing late,
Forgot to write;
I should not wait
'Til morning light.
A poem a day
My goal this year,
A creative way
To bless and cheer,
To raise a talent
To greater heights;
To write of salad
And city lights,
Of sorrowed feelings,
Of joyous grace,
Of daily dealings,
Of a loved one's face.
So though it's late
I'll write a while
Increase my rate,
Improve my style,
In a short time
And day by day
I'll put into rhyme
What I want to say.

Quicksand (2000)

Roiling, violent suction
Under a calm surface –
An innocuous glance rests a little too long
(mistaken for invitation?)
The fate and weight of multitudes unborn
Hangs, balancing.

The Gentle Art of Persuasion (2000)

Mr. Chipper Chopper

With chapped lips

Leaning toward logorrhea

Bends my ear.

Thirst (2000)

Suffering, wounded friend,
You want my cup –
And it would help you, for a while,
But by and by, you know, you'd drink it up,
And I would thirst as well.

Take my hand instead;
Raise yourself up,
Your pain is nearly quenched!
Take the broken cup upon the shelf
And sit here on the bench.

Read along with me...
See, when you reach
In faith, into the Well,
How Living Water rushes, fills the breach
With joy too great to tell!

Thoughts One Long Spring Evening (2000)

I thank the skyreaching treetops
That shelter me,
Cocooning me in pure comfort;
Dried blossoms glide groundward,
Whisking my problems away,
Flying them in the sudden breeze,
Branches sway, they blow away,
Never to return.

Time (2000)

Scarce and scattered schedule slots
I fill up, in haste.
Looks good on paper, and I know
I have no time to waste.
But reading, writing, pondering
Are timeless, quiet things,
And speeding madly to and fro
I can't help wondering
What if, in rush and hurrying
I lose what feeds my soul,
What strengthens talents I may have,
What makes my life feel full?
I do not want to lose those things
In MY life they have place.
Possible mediocrity
In work, I'll bravely face.
Quiet time to think alone
And peaceful time to write
Aare here to stay in my life
My heart knows it's right.

Atonement (2001)

Access to immediate relief
Tenderness beyond belief
Only Son leads us to God
As we grasp the Iron Rod
Every pain borne by the Just
Mingled sweat and blood and dust,
Every woman, every man,
None refused – although we can –
The sacrifice remains.

Breaking Shell (2001)

I am hurt
When he does not regard my creations
With more enthusiasm,
Why do all others view them with awe,
With reverent appreciation –
Yet to him whom I love,
To whom I have given and forgiven
And received kindness and consideration
In every other way,
Why is there but grudged approval
And often disdain and accusal
Of misplaced affection?
It sullies, dulls my joy.
It hinders the development
Of my God-given gifts.
I cannot reach further
If I depend on his approbation,
Yet I am fearful
That the one to whom
My heart is bound
Will reject me completely
If I cut my creative urge
Loose from his opinion:
How I long for a shared rejoicing.

Dog Food (2001)

One day when it came time for lunch,
Young Will sought out dog food to munch.
I asked, half in jest
Which chunks were the best:
He answered, "The gold ones! They crunch!"

Emotional Marathon (2001)

Tight, bubbling fatigue
Ripples through my conscious mind.
All around me spectators, yet no one sees.
The blinded lead, they come away
Shaking heads, they turn aside.
I cannot tell them what it is.
I wish I could; I say words
Not grasped by the listeners,
Which fall uselessly at our feet
Like suffocating crabs, tired butterflies.
The only way out is through,
Apparently.
So my heart crawls on thin, weary legs
To the door.
Yet when I look back,
I have flown or been carried all the way.

Prayer and Study (2001)

"Be not weary in well doing."
The Beloved John and three Nephites
Must have perfected this,
To dwell eternally with the Father.
No motivational tapes -
Faithful prayer and study,
In spite of all difficulty opposing.
Tools lie in my possession that
These men never had.

Love Surrounded Me (2001)

Can you touch the waves of distant waters?
Can you see completely hidden scenes?
You are far away from here, but in my heart
You are now with me.
I can see your eyes, I hear your voice,
Your love surrounds me,
Making burdens lighter
Somehow filling, growing –
How can this be?
As I know the beauty of the morning
Clean and pure and kind,
And gentle as the sun
Shining in a cloudless sky, reminding me
How we want to be.
I can see your eyes, I hear your voice,
Your love surrounds me,
Making burdens lighter
Somehow filling, growing –
So close to me.
Your love surrounded me, surrounded me
Somehow love surrounded me, surrounded me, ah
Your love surrounded me, surrounded me.
So today we'll climb another mountain
Much experience we'll gain, and wisdom too
Every day remembering your love for me,
And my love for you.
I can see your eyes, I hear your voice
Your love surrounds me,
Making burdens lighter
Somehow filling, growing
Eternally.

Storm Warning (2001)

The watchmen on the towers see
Approaching storms, reveal the time
When darkening days come near to me,
Blow out the candle - by design.

They travel on their onward track
They rage and groan and grate and grind
They rush on, never looking back
And seek my hidden place to find.

Help me! I in horror cry
When bitter winds begin to blow,
But in a moment's quiet sigh
Comes hope - and I am safe, I know.

Full moon appears, all creamy white;
The evening stars begin to sing
Soft songs of quiet, peaceful night
And storm's sweet fragrance, lingering.

The Quiet Comes (2001)

Such tumbling life catastrophes
In groups of twos and threes
Rain down on me, upon my life
And bring me to my knees.

Such wondrous, joyful blessings
Such love from God's own heart
Fall down as well, and keep my soul
From ripping clear apart.

Wound (2001)

Buried beneath deep clay
And sandy layers of consciousness
Lies the wound, clean but painful.
Covered daily, hidden well –
But aching grows too great to tell.

Brothers (2001)

Sudden need reveals a brother's love
In faithful kindness, strong directing light,
Wordless hearing what you're thinking of,
Good example showing you what's right.

In faithful kindness, strong directing light,
Sharing skills and helping you be smart
Good example showing you what's right
Mastering in love the friendship art.

Sharing skills and helping you be smart
Letting go, more confidence to give
Mastering in love the friendship art
Offering a place for you to live.

Letting go, more confidence to give
Knowing silence when you start to dream
Offering a place for you to live
When life heats up and trials are extreme

Knowing silence when you start to dream
Wordless hearing what you're thinking of
When life heats up and trials are extreme
Sudden need reveals a brother's love.

He Will Bind Up All Wounds (2002)

Oh my child, my little one,
My stubborn, independent dear;
My precious child, I am here,
My arms around you.
In your pain, your anguished trial,
Do not close the door to love,
To your Father's touch and healing,
But put your faith in Him.
He will bind up all wounds
He will wipe away all tears
He will soften your heart
And remove all fear.
He will bind up all wounds
He will wipe away all tears.
Child, he's given all you need to heal.

Oh my child, His heart is glad
When in gratitude you pray.
When your happy heart remembers
His arms around you.
Share His love and share your joy
With His children everywhere.
Work and serve where He leads you
And put your faith in Him.
He will bind up all wounds
He will wipe away all tears
He will soften your heart
And remove all fear.
He will bind up all wounds
He will wipe away all tears.
Child, he's given all you need to heal.

Progress (2002)

Growth, in tiny increments
Much too small to see
Adds up, with my diligence
To brand-new spankin' me!

Sculpture (2002)

Sometimes I want to whack off weaker parts
Of my character and personality,
But as I do, I see it's not so smart
To mutilate my heart, diminish me.

A lump of clay, chopped fine, is simply dirt –
So, reason dictates, sculpting will produce
Well-rounded strength and beauty without hurt
And make a me much better fit for use.

But how to mend such cracks and flaws as mine?
And what about the pieces on the floor?
My prayer is answered by a love Divine,
A beckoning call to enter at His door.

The Living Water of our Savior's love
Is moisture meant to soften mortal clay,
At any stage of life, to lift above
The shattered, brittle remnants by the way.

If we allow, He gathers, smooths again
Each wandering, dry, degenerating crumb.
By obedience and faith the race of men
May works of art in holiness become.

Dominion (2003)

"I give thee dominion," said the Lord,
Over all the earth, far and wide,
The plants, the beasts and creeping things
And all that lies inside.

Having divine responsibility
Is not the same as control.
It isn't the right to crush and force,
Extinguish, destroy what is whole.

It is the right to order and change,
Tame, nurture, intricately plan,
To beautify, simplify, bring joy to all –
In summary, make God of man.

Success in being like God might result
From learning who God is,
Learning His feelings, His methods and ways,
His perspective on things like this.

In the Bible it says that blessed is he
That cares for his animal's feeling.
The delicate truth of the matter:
Caring brings growth and healing.

Firm caring within embrace of true law
Works miracles in earth, man and beast;
With gentleness, kindness and love unfeigned
From the greatest to the least.

For Bob (2003)

The kindness in your eyes
Is best described
By arched azure skies,
By new-mown grass,
Aged wood kindling friendship's hearth,
Swirling me into a dizzying
New dimension of faith.
Iron barricades evaporate, disappear.
Though stark and still,
My thoughts of you are strangely peaceful, pure.
Wherever life takes me, you are in my heart.
Through you God has purged and closed
Wounds I thought would never heal,
Changing pain to peace and joy,
Laughter comfort and rest.
Thank you.

Miracle of Love (2003)

The air speaks your name
In a profound whisper.
A single drop falls
Into perfectly still water,
Swelling emotion radiates
In circular, soul-filling ripples.
Ebbing, flowing on the shore...

Within the hot, crowded gym
Otherworldly silence
Drowns out basketball din
Affection pours liberally,
Drenching me with joy,
Baptizing me
With strength and renewal,
Healing
My weakness and despair.
Miraculous in its simplicity,
Its fulness complete
In its transforming powers,
Soul-gratifying goodness
Restoring courage and calm.

Your unseen presence
On the endangered bus
Still fills me with awe.

How your complete
But armless embrace
Created a calm cocoon,
A fearless shield,
Even as angry rocks chipped away
At the tinted windows,
And fear dessicated
Those around me.

What miracle is this?
Knowing your thoughts
By spiritual conduit,
Your unspoken words
Reverberate intensely in my mind,
Banishing doubt and fear.

Bob (2004)

If all the worldly chaff would blow away,
We'd see a worthy man, unencumbered
By the pride and foolish notions of our day.
A man as true and pure as finest gold,
Refined by trials, buffeted by pain,
Acute in knowledge, humble, penitent,
Reliant to the core, on heaven bent.
Shining faith in God and love for man,
Patient, tender, kind and generous
Like Jesus Christ, in whom he places trust.

Why does this chaff obscure him
The poverty, the vehicles, and dirt?
To protect him, to preserve him for the time
When the tender hand of God will heal the hurt?
Eternity approaches: does he need
To wait forever lonely in the weeds?
Life's irony of trial is manifest
In placing out of reach the very best.
To eternity's horizon I am drawn,
To a vast and glorious sunset, pink and gold,
The silver sparkling clouds now herald dawn,
Where none weep lonely tears nor men grow old.

The golden road will appear presently,
But what to do for now, most urgently
Presses in my mind, how to proceed,
To walk away from him in time of need?
For me, he answers every need I know,
But he hesitates, and I am called to go.
And like an unripe fruit, a something green
And undeveloped lingers in between.
Perfect love is not possession, as I see:
His shortest path to growth is not to be with me
The choreography of God in this love dance
Will allow us each a precious chance
To strengthen and develop on our own,
To serve and know our God as we are known.
When God allows, directs, we may proceed,
We'll find that He in mercy met each need.
He straightened every tangle, set all straight
Because we let Him lead, willing to wait.

Feed My Sheep (2004)

Firmly rooted rod of iron;
Yawning gulf along the narrow road
Beckoning hands as I reach the tree.
Dusk is falling, precious souls wander,
Even those who once tasted –
Who knowingly reject exquisite fruit
With sweetness filling every need.
The faithful are puzzled, watching them fall,
Unable to rescue without straying too far.
Lost amid the shuffle:
Little lambs whose parents lost their way.
Innocently wrong – so many in our day
Who tasted once, who tried to reach,
But slid or stumbled back, how dear is each
To pleading Shepherd:
None escapes His view.

To Idaho (2004)

Allons, enfants, the time has come to go,
To pack our junk and move to Idaho,
To leave the dear degenerating place behind,
To set out fresh, a better life to find.
Though very sorry now you are to go
In faith, you'll find good folks to love, I know.
Great opportunities to grow and build your mind
Refreshing purpose, work and joy divine.
Come along then, go to and work with me.
Celebrate this fine new opportunity.

Summer Arbor (2004)

Equidistant stars
Balance prettily over the bedspread sky
Winking slyly at the lovers
Gazing at the moon
From a sturdy arbor
A local artist whipped up
Out of potato grubbers, rebar
And machinery cogs, sun-shaped,
Its rusted glory echoing
The brilliant, burning purity
Of June roses blooming
And love's first kiss.

Trusting in Thee (2004)

I have trusted in my Lord
When He has put me in a boat
At night, without oars,
To sit alone on the lake,
Safe in the knowledge
That at any moment
He can walk across the deep
Or bid me to Him.

I have trusted in my Lord
When he has directed me to climb at dawn
To a rocky, inaccessible cliff
And there wait for Him
To come on wings of eagles,
When He asks that I step off the edge
Of known security
Into His unseen arms.

I have trusted in my Lord,
Waited long years faithfully
Amidst grief and disappointment,
Enduring cruel perversions
And torturous ironies;
And when I could go no further in the darkness,
He placed a lamp of eternal love
To light my path forever.

For long years I have known He will come,
He will fulfill His works, no mortal hand

Can stay the tumbling stone.
No unhallowed plan
Can reach His majestic throne.

Even if I am but driftwood,
Merely flotsam on His pond,
His eternal purposes,
His magnificent Fatherhood
Encompass me and make me whole.
His loving hand blesses me.

I wait upon His will.
Where is there room in my heart
To receive His magnificent blessings?
To comprehend His immortal glory?
I see the glimmering stars,
The towering pines, and am reminded
Of His eyes ever upon me,
Of His matchless strength
Of His greatness and goodness
Beyond all understanding.

See The Angel Fly (2005)

In the cloud on the mountain, we come home to you.
With mist all around, we walk free
Quiet grass on the hillside and sparkling dew
Grace the path as we come near to Thee.
Wintry darkness was chill, and we traveled alone
'Til your voice called and showed us the way
To fresh fountains of joy, peace and love never known,
To inner light brighter than day!
Higher we climb in our journey,
Light gently shines through the lies;
The clear voice of peace stills the trembling
Love lifts our weary hearts up to the skies
To the crystal reflections, visions of glory –
Look! See the Angel fly!
Look! See the Angel fly!

Where the sea of humanity breaks on the shores
Of eternal relief, we must go –
Quickly lift from cold waves and lead to the warm sand
Of fellowship and love that we know.
Higher we climb in our journey,
Light gently shines through the lies;
The clear voice of peace stills the trembling
Love lifts our weary hearts up to the skies
To the crystal reflections, visions of glory –
Look! See the Angel fly!
See the mighty Angel fly!
See the mighty Angel, the mighty Angel fly!

Softly (2004)

Endless wells of love, your eyes
Speaking blessings from above
Knowing as I do that we can build
How can I leave?

My life, my will are not my own
But belong to Him who died for me.

Someday soon, see the moon,
And remember He is near.
Softly now, remember how
I love you.

Remarkable (2004)

Remarkable praise
To a yellow-robed man
For diluted counsel,
However bland.
Ten thousand pay
To see the man, His Holiness.
But Man of Holiness speaks anew
To living prophet wise and true.
Thousands watch
And humbly walk
In wisdom's rich but thorny ways.
Sometimes his loving words are hard
On sin, and those who disregard
Must wait.

Warm Butter (2004)

Churned vigorously,
Sharp imperfections,
Lateral angles rounded, cleansed
Seeping, slowly softening.

Profound reshaping,
Molding, cooling,
Sculpted to a delicate flower
Iced in a tray
And stabbed and scraped
By knives at the banquet.

You Just Remind Me (2004)

You just remind me
Of what I thought I was getting
When I got something terribly different
Brilliant integrity
Positive intensity
I still miss it,
Even though I never had it.
Do not fear me.
All will be right in the end.
I want nothing of yours,
But let me look a little longer.
Do not let me distract you.
You just remind me.

You've Come All This Way (2004)

You've come all this way,
Left the old life behind,
Learned a new way of living,
And you're healthy today.
Was it strange, going back
To the friends you once knew
In the old life? Was it difficult
To be there, for you?
Did you stand in resolve,
Letting progress prevail?
Did you slip and give in,
Or otherwise fail?
I hope all went well, Chris,
There's so much unseen,
So much that is worthy in you,
Know what I mean?

The Child Within (2004)

The child within says,
Thank you for letting me speak.
Radiant harmonies rise up
In anticipation of birth,
Your devoting time to me, listening,
Lets them come forth
In sunny landscapes, rainy nights,
Blissful moments of pure delight.
They crowd near the vestibule,
Making everyday traffic inconvenient.
Prepare yourself with tools.
Pens, paper, time allotted,
And come ready to write
With the passion and fury
Of wild horses and thunderstorms,
With all of the wisdom
Of your eyes and mind.
And Spirit – oh yes.
Call upon the joys and sorrows,
The anger, contentment, resentment,
Resolve to tell their stories.
Let the ancestors speak
From their faraway times
Let them live again through you.
They want to be heard –
Many lessons can be drawn from
The bare facts of their lives
Now in your possession.
What are you waiting for?

Cold (2004)

Stuffy nose, wracking cough
Three weeks out, a little rough.
When I think I'm gonna sneeze
Attribute to those allergies.
Keep Kleenex in business.

Time (2004)

Time is relative.
Why else are the busiest people
Also those who can take on a job
And finish it in short order,
While those with apparent time
Lack efficiency, motivation, or something
And cannot do it?

Debbie (2004)

Perhaps it is time now to write
What you did to me;
To release the anger, the hurt
Buried all these years.
Why did you do it?
Now it is understandable
But then it was not.
Why, when we had shared every recess,
Vacations, summers, weekends
For five years
Did you suddenly become unenthused,
Even embarrassed with me?
Maybe it was the day I belly-flopped
Into the campground pool
With your older cousins looking on.
The pool, I recall, was swarmed with ladybugs,
Cute little things crawling on my shoulder.
Or maybe when I grew long and awkward
And my confidence flagged.
Perhaps it was just the fact
That we were no longer in the same class.
I think you did not know, you never did
How profound was my loneliness;
You were mostly distracted.
But I forgive you.
I do have pleasant memories
Your little parakeet landing on my head,
Your fish, and your father teasing,

Your mother's pleasing efficiency.
I want to remember those things.
I am thankful for the strength and experience
That those difficult years gave me.
It was not a total loss.
But the timing was unfortunate.
Puberty's usual issues
And a lack of other friends
Made it hard to replace your companionship
For several years, especially
When brother Jeffrey died,
Sweet John as well.
My social graces
Are still a little rusty and pained -
Ah, friend, it was unfortunate.
Let love prevail.
God will heal all hurts.
Release...
Let the pain and anger flow out
My mouth, my heart, my feet,
Like flocks of birds, black and white,
Chirping softly to each other.
Let the warmth of forgiveness
And understanding
Envelop me, assure me.
My life has taken the path
The Father wanted for me.
His blessings are more than
Compensation
For petty pain.
I love you, Debbie.

Why Patience? (2004)

Why patience?
Trying to have it,
Having it tried.
Sometimes I don't want to,
But it often equals strength.

Mind Wash (2006)

Thanks to David

I am so full
Of love, of anger, of frustration, of peace,
Flowing turmoil, a riotous mixture
That renders me somewhat
Numb, unable to focus,
Or take each individually, examining the content.
I plod and muddle amid blended lights and darks,
Black sweaters turning white linens gray –
Unsatisfied, unexpressed, sorrowing,
Working and waiting for time to be sane.
It insufficiently arrives,
Trickling like water through my fingers,
Wasted.
I grasp in a murk of emotion,
Desperate for relief.
A strong, gentle voice speaks
Clarity and caring, lifting me to see
Above the cloud for a moment...
Pure rinsings of thought, washed by rain from above
O Blessed contrast!
Lift me again! My thirst is not slaked,
Even by daily drinking.
Wisdom whispers patience, caution as
Unfulfilled dreams crowd forward hasty, hungry.

Thanks to Paul (2006)

Appearing in sudden gusts of trial,
Some friends are delivering angels,
Transforming from acquaintances or enemies,
Some friends are surprises,
Traveling in a common plane of experience,
Some friends are only linked by circumstance.
But you...
Speaking your beautiful prose,
Walking beside my inner mind,
Somehow familiar –
And not exactly unexpected;
Your presence in my life whispers
Peace and assurance in my very secret trials.
Your life, your vision and understanding
Have refocused my mind and spirit,
Engaging me in the higher walk
I have been striving for,
Dropping burdens I have held too closely.
Your generous, holy ways comfort me.
Thank you.

Friendship (2006)

My bitter thirst is slaked
With friendship's dew.
The pouring forth of pent-up thoughts
And a soothing night's rest
With soft-feathered smiles
And twigs of tenderness
We build a safe nest
Where fears and sorrows
Are forgotten.

Promise (2007)

Wheat's golden sunlit glow
Deep cerulean blue summer dusk
And waving, verdant green
Unite in vision.
But a painful ache of absence
Casts a thin pall, a cloud
On the bright, blissful day.
A black fly of fear
Crawls along
The diamond joy
Of discovery.

Endurance (2007)

End it tonight – it must end!
Or take root
In some insidious form
I want no part of.
Away with doubt, fears,
The pangs and sorrows
Of forty-six years.
I lay them at His feet,
Give up my heart to His hands
And, as He bids me, I rejoice!
No harm will come of reaching out.
I have lost NOTHING.
I have gained peace, love,
Friendship, knowledge,
And the ineffable sense
Of having done good.
Rise up, Zion, and walk
Shed the tattered robes,
The minimizing thoughts;
Put on the beautiful garments,
The freshness of love and faith.
Walk calmly, if not quickly,
Deliberately joyful, serene
Amid chaos and life's turns.
Others sorrow too
And can be comforted
By my endurance now.
Press on.

www.ingramcontent.com/pod-product-compliance
Lightning Source LLC
Chambersburg PA
CBHW050153110726
47898CB00008B/2785

* 9 7 8 1 7 3 2 2 4 1 2 4 4 *